MAGNETISM

Christopher Forest and John Willis

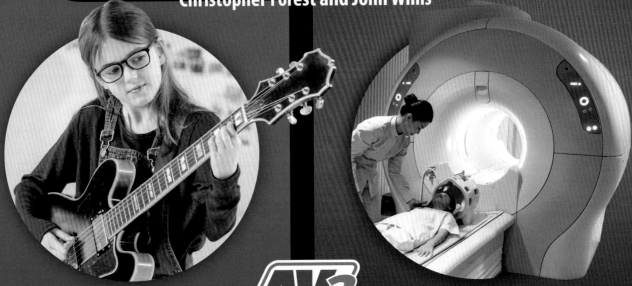

AV2

www.av2books.com

Step 1
Go to **www.av2books.com**

Step 2
Enter this unique code

EPNYCAWU0

Step 3
Explore your interactive eBook!

CONTENTS

AV2 is optimized for use on any device

Your interactive eBook comes with...

Contents
Browse a live contents page to easily navigate through resources

Audio
Listen to sections of the book read aloud

Videos
Watch informative video clips

Weblinks
Gain additional information for research

Try This!
Complete activities and hands-on experiments

Key Words
Study vocabulary, and complete a matching word activity

Quizzes
Test your knowledge

Slideshows
View images and captions

... and much, much more!

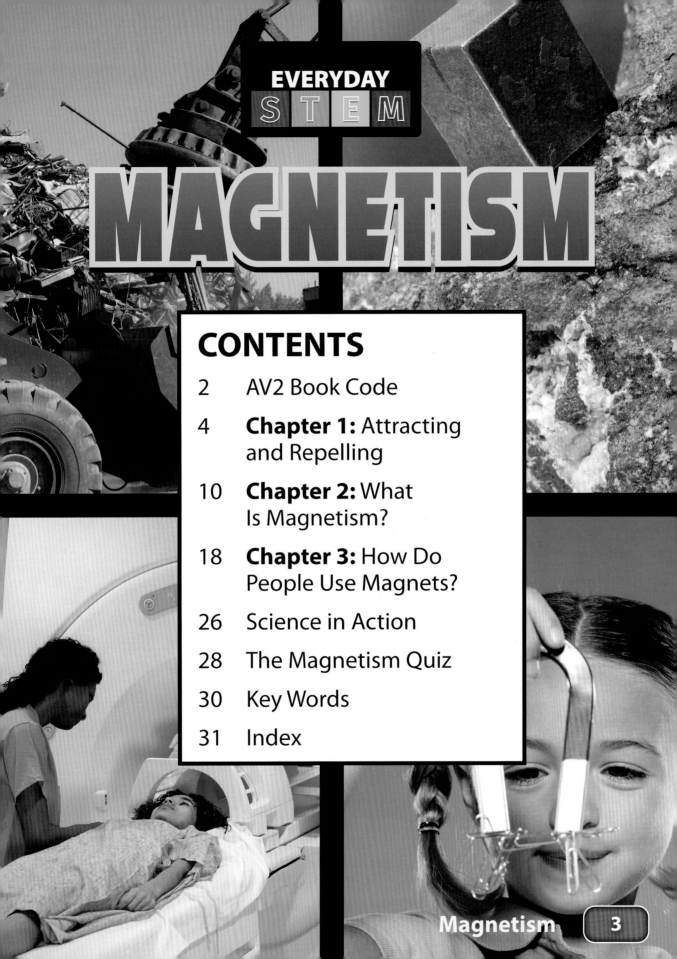

EVERYDAY STEM

MAGNETISM

CONTENTS

Attracting and Repelling

J ose finishes a drawing that he is very proud of. He wants to put the drawing where his whole family will see it. He holds the drawing against the refrigerator. Then, he puts a magnet on top of it.

The magnet clings to the refrigerator. It holds the drawing in place. Why does the magnet stick to the refrigerator? This happens because the refrigerator is made of a magnetic metal. Magnets are **attracted** to these metals. That means magnets are pulled toward them. Not all metals are magnetic, but many are.

Everyday STEM

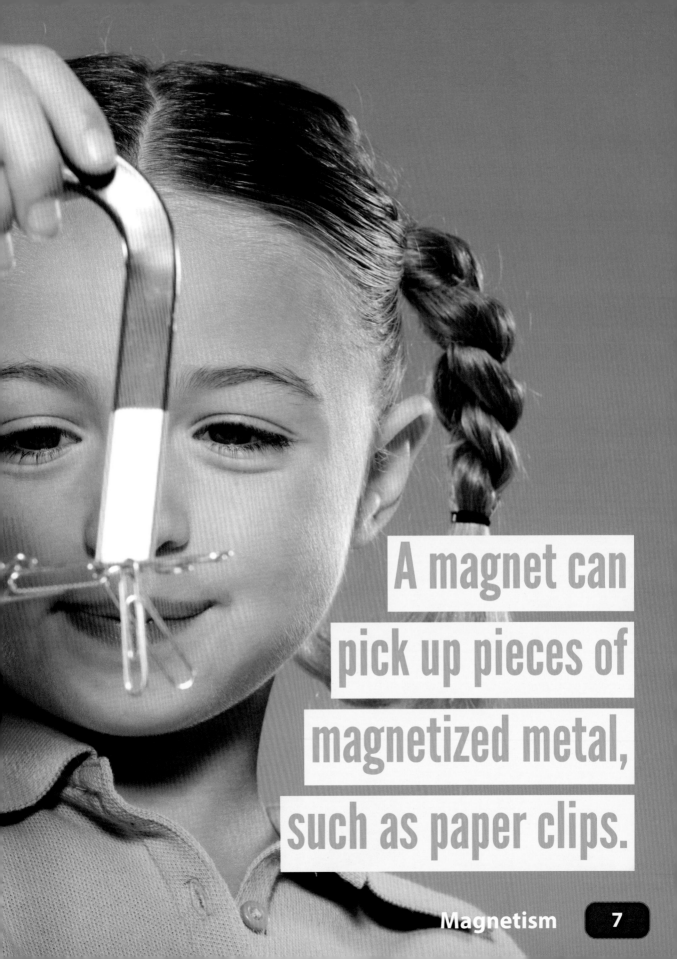

A magnet can pick up pieces of magnetized metal, such as paper clips.

A strong magnet can pull another magnet off the table.

Now Jose reaches into a drawer. He grabs two more magnets. He holds the ends close to one another. This time, he cannot make the magnets stay together. The ends of the magnets **repel** one other. This means the magnets push apart.

Magnets can either repel or attract. It depends upon how they are lined up. Magnets are an important part of our lives. Many people use them every day.

What Is Magnetism?

Humans have been using magnets for thousands of years. In ancient times, people saw that pieces of iron could stick to lodestones. Lodestones are stones that contain iron.

Lodestones attract other pieces of iron. They can even magnetize steel. Lodestones may have seemed like magic to ancient people. Over time, however, scientists learned that lodestones are magnetic.

Magnetized steel strings allow an electric guitar to make music.

A magnet is an object that has a magnetic field around it. A magnetic field is invisible, but it may cause nearby objects to feel a force. The magnetic field may push or pull.

A magnetic field is caused by moving electric charges. **Atoms** are the building blocks of the objects around us. Atoms contain electric charges called **electrons**.

Electrons are always in motion. Their motion creates a magnetic field. The magnetic field of one magnet can cause a force on a nearby magnet.

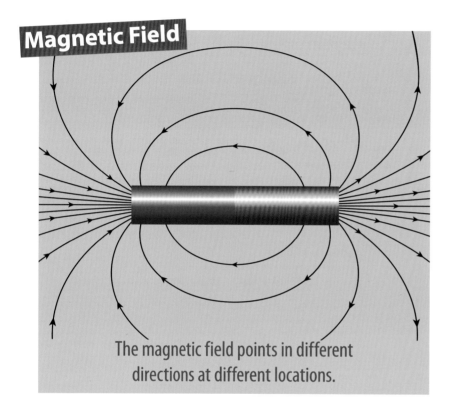

Magnetic Field

The magnetic field points in different directions at different locations.

Iron and nickel are two examples of magnetic metals. They are found in many everyday objects. For example, car parts and frying pans are often made of iron. Wires, machines, and coins are often made of nickel.

Everyday STEM

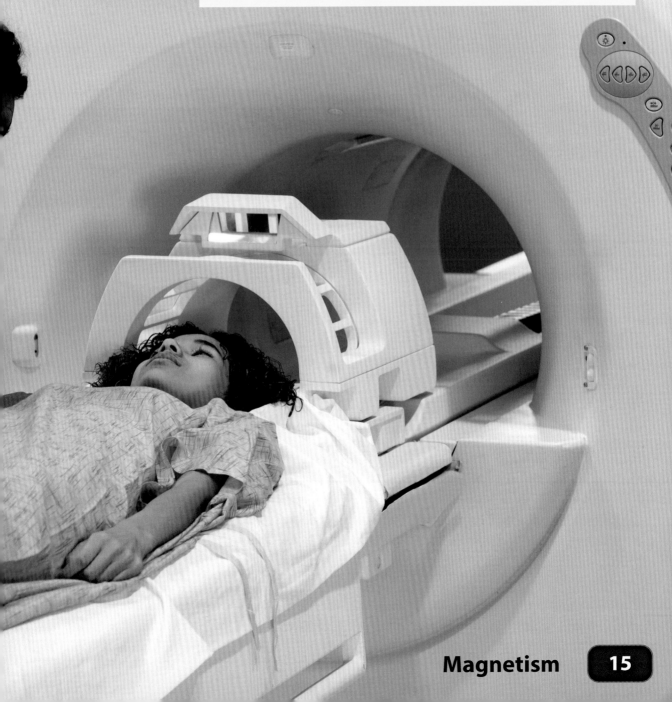

Doctors use magnetic fields to see inside our bodies.

Magnets have **poles**. Magnetic field lines come out near the magnet's north pole. The lines go in near the magnet's south pole. These field lines never cross.

Magnets can be attracted by other magnets. The north pole of one magnet is attracted to the south pole of another magnet.

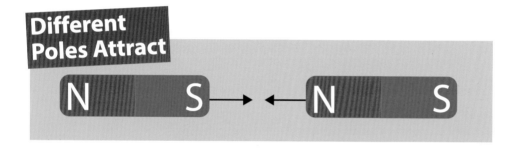

However, the north pole of one magnet repels the north pole of another magnet. The south poles of two magnets also repel.

MAGNETIC POLES

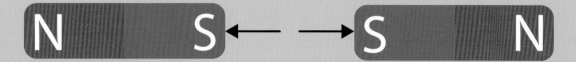

The south poles of two magnets repel.

The south pole of one magnet and
the north pole of another magnet attract.

The north poles of two magnets repel.

How Do People Use Magnets?

Magnets have many uses. Sometimes, they are used to make objects stay together. This is how a refrigerator door stays closed. One magnet is in the refrigerator. Another magnet Is In the door. The two magnets are attracted to one another. They cause the door to pull itself shut.

Junkyard magnets can help separate magnetic and non-magnetic metals.

A magnet can also be used to keep objects attached to metal. For example, many schools have magnetic whiteboards. Teachers can attach papers to these boards with magnets.

Some magnets make life easier for workers. Junkyard owners use large machines with powerful magnets on them. These machines help them move heavy cars.

Sanitation companies use magnets when moving trash. Their magnets pull metal out of trash. The metal can be recycled. Many computers also rely on magnets. The magnets in a computer help store information.

Magnets can be used for travel, too. For example, some trains have large magnets instead of wheels. The tracks also have magnets. The two magnets repel. So, the train does not touch the tracks. Instead, the train rides above the tracks. Magnetic trains can travel at very high speeds.

Some trains that use magnets can reach speeds of 310 miles per hour (500 kilometers per hour).

Compasses can help people who are hiking.

People also use magnets to help with directions. Earth has its own magnetic field. That means our planet acts like a giant magnet. A **compass** uses a magnet, too. The magnet points toward one of Earth's poles. The poles are north and south. This helps people figure out which way to go.

Long ago, magnets seemed like magical objects. Today, they are no longer a mystery. They make life simpler for everyone.

Make a Magnet

What will happen if you rest a steel nail against a magnet? Perform this experiment to find out. Be sure to get help from an adult.

STEP 1 Get a screwdriver that is not magnetized. Get a nail made of steel, too.

STEP 2 Touch the nail to the screwdriver. Watch what happens to the nail.

STEP 3 Now get a magnet, and place it on the table.

STEP 4 Rest the nail against one end of the magnet. Allow the nail to rest on the magnet for about five minutes.

STEP 5 Remove the nail. Place the nail next to the screwdriver again. What do you notice? Did the nail behave differently after it rested on the magnet? How can you explain what happened? What would happen if you rested the nail against the magnet for only one minute? What if you rested it for 30 minutes?

THE MAGNETISM QUIZ

- 1 -
Are all metals magnetic?

A. No

- 2 -
What do magnets do when they repel?

A. Push apart

- 3 -
Can you see a magnetic field?

A. No

- 4 -
What are lodestones?

A. Stones that contain iron

- 5 -
Is nickel a magnetic metal?

A. Yes

- 6 -

What does the movement of electrons create?

A. A magnetic field

- 7 -

Do like poles attract or repel?

A. Repel

- 8 -

Can powerful magnets lift heavy cars?

A. Yes

- 9 -

Does a magnetic train touch the tracks?

A. No

- 10 -

What magnetic device helps hikers find their way?

A. A compass

Key Words

atoms: tiny units of matter that most of the objects around us are made of

attracted: pulled toward

compass: a tool that uses a needle to show direction

electrons: charged particles that can be in atoms or on their own

poles: the points where the magnetic field lines enter and leave a magnet

repel: to push away from

sanitation: having to do with removing trash

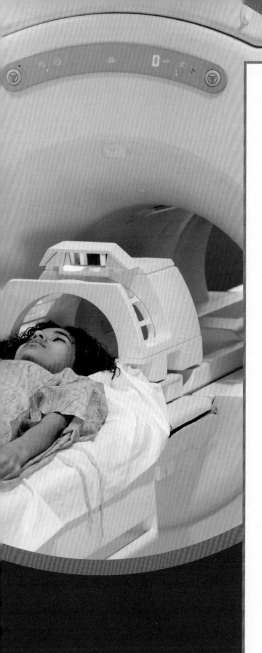

Index

Get the best of both worlds.

AV2 bridges the gap between print and digital.

The expandable resources toolbar enables quick access to content including **videos**, **audio**, **activities**, **weblinks**, **slideshows**, **quizzes**, and **key words**.

Animated videos make static images come alive.

Resource icons on each page help readers to further **explore key concepts**.

Published by AV2
14 Penn Plaza, 9th Floor New York, NY 10122
Website: www.av2books.com

Library of Congress Control Number: 2020936969

ISBN 978-1-7911-2384-0 (hardcover)
ISBN 978-1-7911-2385-7 (softcover)
ISBN 978-1-7911-2386-4 (multi-user eBook)
ISBN 978-1-7911-2387-1 (single-user eBook)

Printed in Guangzhou, China
1 2 3 4 5 6 7 8 9 0   24 23 22 21 20

052020
101319

Designer: Terry Paulhus Project Coordinator: Priyanka Das

Every reasonable effort has been made to trace ownership and to obtain permission to reprint copyright material. The publisher would be pleased to have any errors or omissions brought to its attention so that they may be corrected in subsequent printings.

The publisher acknowledges Getty Images and Shutterstock as its primary image suppliers for this title.

First published by Focus Readers in 2018.